DICHTEN =
No. FOUR

No. 1: Friederike Mayröcker, *Heiligenanstalt*, 1994
No. 2: Elke Erb, *Mountains in Berlin*, 1995
No. 3: Ilma Rakusa, *Steppe*, 1997
No. 4: Ernst Jandl, *reft and light*, 2000

# reft and light

Poems by Ernst Jandl
with Multiple Versions by American Poets

BURNING DECK, PROVIDENCE
2000

DICHTEN = is a (not quite) annual of current German writing in English translation. Most issues are given to the work of a single author. Editor: Rosmarie Waldrop.

Individual copies: $10
Subscription for 2 issues: $16
In England: £5.
Subscription for 2 issues: £8. Postage 25p/copy.

Distributors:
Small Press Distribution, 1341 Seventh St., Berkeley, CA 94710
1-800/869-7553; orders@spdbooks.org
Spectacular Diseases, c/o Paul Green, 83b London Rd., Peterborough, Cambs. PE2 9BS

for US subscriptions only:
Burning Deck, 71 Elmgrove Ave., Providence RI 02906

The texts in this volume are taken from the following collections: *laut und luise*, 1966; *sprechblasen*, 1968; *der künstliche baum*, 1970; *übung mit buben*, 1973; *wischen möchten*, 1974; *der gelbe hund*, 1980; *idyllen*, 1992. Some of Rosmarie Waldrop's translations were first printed in *The Vienna Group: 6 Major Austrian Poets*, Station Hill Press, 1985.

ISSN 1077-4203
ISBN 1-8862224-34-x

Burning Deck is the literature program of Anyart: Contemporary Arts Center, a tax-exempt non-profit corporation.

Cover by Keith Waldrop

# REFT AND LIGHT

**dilection**

some think
terring reft flom light
is a piece of cake.
boy are they evel
long!

Anselm Hollo

Editor's note:

Most of Ernst Jandl's poems are so engrained in the German language that they are  impossible to translate. But their procedures can be imitated. Here is an experiment: several American poets respond to each poem so that the original is encircled by multiple English analogues. The responses (which range from close imitations to freewheeling versions that continue Jandl's thinking into other semantic areas) form the first part of this book. The version that seems closest to Jandl's text is usually the first to follow the German.

Part II presents, in roughly  chronological order, poems by Ernst Jandl either left in their original form (including visual poems and poems that he wrote in English) or translated/adapted by Anselm Hollo or myself.

Rosmarie Waldrop

# CONTENTS

# I
# ENCIRCLINGS

hosi


anna
maria
magdalena

  hosi


      hosianna
      hosimaria
      hosimagdalena

        hosinas


            hosiannanas
            hosimarianas
            hosmagdalenanas


ananas


                      E. J.

**hosp**


nya nya
rammed
nelly fag gam

    hosp


        hosp nya nya
        hosp rammed
        hosp nelly fag gam

          hosp ass


                hosp nya nya ass
                hosp rammed ass
                hosp nelly fag gam ass


aspirin


Kenward Elmslie

12

**thee-three**


anna
maria
magdalena

thee-three unmentionables


tight-lipped anna
close-mouthed maria
mum magdalena

thee tight-lipped trio


tight anna-lipped
close-maria mouthed
mumagdalenam


three undeparted


Ray Ragosta

13

**anna**


soror
sorry
anna

   vergilannex


          manyanna
          mamamia
          mamigotti

            annagotti


                  manyzanax
                  sorryverdi
                  moneyapplesinner


annex


                     Norma Cole

**ave banana**


ave banana


ave hosanna hosea banana hose anna and eve

    hose a banana an adamant eve

    hosa banana    adam meant eve    anna meant eve

        anna and eve
        add um banana

hosanna banana hosea hosadam hosanna hoseve


Joan Retallack

# BESSEMERBIRNEN

## als mehr kanonen

E. J.

["Bessemer" sounds very much like *besser mehr*, "better more," and the converter used in the Bessemer steel-making process is called *Birne*, "pear," for its shape.]

BETTER TO BURN
than anything more canonical

Ray DiPalma

BETTEREADYME
than more batter

Norma Cole


BRING OUT THE HELLMAN'S
and fling out the helmets

Lori Baker & Gale Nelson


CANONINCAMERA
trumps simulacra

BETTEREADYOU
than soufflé

Gale Nelson

Norma Cole


BURN
ING PEAR
CANON WE
LIVED LIGHT-PEARS
AWAY FROM MORE LIGHT
THAN HEAT ATE BLIGHTED
PEARS OF MORE HATE THAN
LIGHT  LOST  SIGHT  OF  PEAR-
LIGHT IN BENIGHTED SLIGHTS
*B E S S E M E R B I R N E N*
*als  mehr  kanonen*

Joan Retallack

17

Bessemer Weltanschauung.com
at the behest of delicatessen not guns

Bessemer Weltanschauung.com
with delicatessen in sites not guns

Bessemer Weltanschauung.com
possessive of macaroni not guns

Would word wild wold weltanschauung.com
welcome advert-constructor!

Bessemer Blast! Furnish
warmer welcome to guest

Bessemer Weltanschauung.com
sent guest warm welcome

Would Bessemer Furnish
alter-native thermos

BASTIAN BLESSING
cannot bless cannon

BASTION BLESSING
acanonically

B(L)ASTIAN BLESSING
bastion. Send word.

B(L)ASTIAN BLESSING
bastion acanonically

BASTIAN BLESSING
wearing blender

BASTIAN BLESSING
earing on ear no war

BASTIAN BLESSING
wounds not cannon

NOTES:
the Bessemer
converter is a
furnace prob-
ably univer-
sally known.

"Welcome"
derives from
words mean-
ing "desirable
guest."

Bastian
Blessing is
an electrical
soda fountain
mixer.

Marjorie Welish

18

reihe

eis
zweig
dreist
vieh
füllf
ächz
silben
ach
neu
zink

## series

wan
too
tree
fur
fife
sics
severance
ate
nein
tin

Benjamin Friedlander

## series

once
toil
threne
furculum
fife
signet
senna
eidolon
night
tend

Laynie Browne

## series

wand
toot
tree
fort
fry
sex
servin'
eh
none
tan

Martine Bellen

## down the line

won
toot
treat
for
fife
sex
several
ate
nylon
tense

Keith Waldrop

## reihe

I bin see de effigy.
Hey, chide jake, eh?
Hell! I'm in no pique—
you are as thee you be.
Double your acts.
Why's he—done?

Elizabeth MacKiernan

| cherries | ceres | seers | jerries | cerise |
|---|---|---|---|---|
| rung | numb | rum | runt | hun |
| dew | true | chew | dude | toot |
| tree | gris | dray | treat | teat |
| fear | veer | fire | freak | fork |
| vibe | fife | fink | flyte | fight |
| sex | zyxt | cigs | styx | snits |
| seaman | semen | sheba | zebulon | savon |
| hatch | ace | ox | ape | ache |
| gnome | nun | nix | knife | niche |
| den | zen | zing | djinn | sin |

Ray DiPalma

| hind | hide | iron | ice |
|---|---|---|---|
| size | wine | side | sign |
| wire | dry | ride | triune |
| fear | for | fear | fire |
| fund | fun | fount | funnel |
| sexy | except | except | sack |
| bent | seepin' | syllable | secret |
| act | out | hex | hark |
| anoint | 'nuff | noun | noise |
| zen | said | zine | sang |

Julie Patton

# series

on

to

tree

for

I've  sick

even     ate

brine          tench

                       Lytle Shaw

# Serieses

| win | wan | tan | sun | than | done | pun | ton | bun |
|---|---|---|---|---|---|---|---|---|
| lose | galoot | coot | soon | moot | noose | lose | too | loose |
| tree | trees | free | see | free | free | me | knee | we |
| flower | fart | fart | soar | hour | nor | more | wore | tour |
| thrive | naïve | slime | slime | I've | live | hive | pine | live |
| hex | sex | sex | sex | sox | nix | hicks | clicks | fix |
| heaven | revenge | heaven | stoopid | leaven | never | never | ascend | maven |
| mate | abate | bait | sate | wait | fate | late | pate | sate |
| mine | none | none | swine | mine | whine | sign | climb | wine |
| bend | ken | ken | spend | then | then | when | mend | hen |

James Sherry

                       22

canzone

ganz
ganz
        ohne


völlig beraubt


canzone


ganz
ganz
        ohne


völlig beraubt




E. J.

**canzone**

|  | **canzone** | **canzone** |
|---|---|---|
| and | | |
| and | | |
|   zone | o | o |
| | o | o |
| none whatsoever | zone | zaum |
| | at sea | continuo |
| canzone | | |
| and | canzone | canzone |
| and | | |
|   zone | o | o |
| | o | o |
| none whatsoever | zone | zaum |
| | at sea | continuo |

**canzone**

    canto
    canto
      antiseptic

un deux sept huit

    canzone

    canto
    canto
      antiseptic

un deux sept huit

Marjorie Welish

**medieval**

                                                           **plainchant**

'mid
'mid
    evil

                                                           plane

               **madrigal**               plane

no good                                                   slant

               sadly

medieval               sadly                       orbit revolve

                   full

'mid                                                   plainchant
'mid               wholly undone
    evil

                                                       plane

               madrigal               plane

no good                                                   slant

               sadly

               sadly                       orbit revolve

                   full

               wholly undone

                                                   Gale Nelson

**can zone**

goose egg
goose egg
    nada

totally ripped-off

                **a little song**
can zone

                can't zone it
goose egg
goose egg
    nada          canned
                canned
                    oh no

totally ripped-off

                brillig sursauts

        Ray DiPalma

                cans own

                the game
                gained
                    one

                slithey somersaulting brillig

                    Cole Swensen

## der und die

kam der und die kam und die kam vor ihm ins tal und
das war der ort und die sah hin und her und tat das
oft und war müd und bös und wie eis und sah hin und
her bis der kam der ins tal kam und nun los und das
eis weg und der kam und der kam nah und kam ihr nah
und war bei ihr und war nah bei ihr und sah auf ihr
hin und her und die war wie für ihn war für ihn ist
was für ihn ist muß mit und den hut und wie der den
zog und zog aug bei aug auf ihr hin und her und ihr
kam der ist wie ein ist was das ist was das ist für
uns nun los und gib wie das eis weg süß und küß bis
ans end der uhr und tag aus aug und ohr weg nur gut
und naß und süß tau mit rum und nun los bot den arm
und gab ihm den und das ohr und das auf und süd und
ost und zog mit ihr mit ihm mit und das tor war los
und die tür und der tag weg mit eis und müd und wut
und hut und der ihr und die ihm und sog kuß aus kuß
und hob und lud sie auf das ist gut ist für uns und
los und ihn biß und der riß und zog und die ihn und
bot ihm naß und süß tau mit rum und sog was der und
der lag auf ihr und zog und tat und riß und biß und
sog und ihr arm und das auf süd und das ohr die tür
zur see und das amt aus und tot und wer vor mir ist
weg ost weg nur ich auf hin und her hin und hun her
hin her hin her bis rot und süß und wut die see ins
tal riß und goß und den ort naß und müd lag auf uns

E. J.

# bop and buy

```
bag bop and buy bag and bop bag for his sun lad and
sad war dry rot and buy has him and her and tot sad
fft and war mud and sob and why ice and has him and
her bud bop bag bop sun lad bag and not old and sad

ice wig and bop bag and bop bag nah and bag hid nah
and war boy hid and war nah boy hid and has oof hid
him and her and buy war him fat hen war fat hen sit
saw fat hen sit bum dim and den hut and why bop den

zig and zig gee boy gee oof hid him and her and hid
bag bop sit why one sit bad sad sit bad sad sit fat
sin not old and big why sad ice wig dip and rip bad
lib fit bop rut and dig big sag and sue how now git

and nap and dip hot bit mum and not old tug den rim
and gab dim den and sad pad and sad rug and low and
sit and zig bit hid bit his bit and sad rap war old
and buy gat and bop rat wig bit ice and mud and air

and hut and bop hid and buy his and god rip and rip
and bob and lug sod off sad sit out sit fat sin and
old and hen pit and bop rib and zig and buy hen and
pat tip nap and bus hot bit mum and god sad bop and

bop leg oof hid and zig and tag and rib and bib and
gag and hid arm and sad gee dad and sad sue buy bra
zoo sea and sad tab big and dug and are raw rim hot
veg sat wed not hip oof him and her him and him her

him her him her bad dot and dip and who buy see sun
lad rib and bob and den rut gyp and mud lag oof sin
```

Kenward Elmslie

### dew and die

```
can dew and die can and die can tie his sin tap and
the war dew hoe and die has him and her and tar the
pry and war mud and bog and tug eye and has him and
her bug dew can dew sin tap can and not lie and the
eye wag and the can and the can not and can ire not
and war beg ire and war not beg ire and has out ire
him and her and die war tug for kin war for kin its
was for kin its mob tic and ken hot and tug dew ken
sob and sob hog beg hop for ire him and tug dew ken
can dew its tug art its was the its was the its for
sun not lie and gag tug the eye wag sub and hug but
pun end dew oar and tag irk hog and our wag nor gut
and nab and sub top tic rum and not lie pop ken arm
and gab his ken and the our and the hog and sad and
sit and sob tic ire tic his tic and the rot war lie
and die rut and dew tag wag tic eye and mud and woe
and not and dew ire and die his and sow hug irk hug
and hit and lug tie out the its gut its for sun and
lie and kin bob and dew rib and sob and die kin and
bug his nab and sub top tic rum and sow was dew and
dew lay out ire and sob and tar and rib and bob and
sow and ire arm and the hog sad and the our die rut
zen see and the amp irk and tot and wet for rim its
wag sit wag nor she out him and her him and him her
him her him her big rot and sob and woe die see sin
tap rib and bob and ken orb nab and mud lag out sun
```

Charles Bernstein

# not set all set

his not set yet and her all set now yet due for cue
and cue set for his icy eye and her ear not duo now
yet her far out kin ebb his rue our dud and her ebb
not all set now was fit for her mug and got his aft
age ago all set yet not the set for sax ebb had got
his off her nub and icy eye now got him off his nut
lit the set for shy ace and fed her fit way too rip
his too zig and zag for the duo bug her kin not set
yet fat cat got his nod off bar and now bar his way
the gap too bum cue not set and lop off the old leg
all set one eon ago one age ago say fry the vow say
let rip its sub sad run bit off key duo due too low
she who can set rut off end and box his ear yet ply
her lam for key and bud the icy eye its gem now kin
née shy ace his bur set aft who got the wad guy bit
and got her icy eye ebb off its row and saw his eve
rag ear and egg the gut for our dud and rip his fig
not set for the few who set his arc off ear and hid
its nub set its gem out for her far out kin our ebb
our run aft and off its nod out the axe his icy eye
let rip its bug off and beg off and fry the fit dry
lop off its cap her nod off wry and dug far aft and
now bar its dry duo due for hew and cry out cut off
his way out fit the cue not for our ebb sax run née
fat cat sub any arc any dub his cue for his icy eye
all set now and her ear not set yet for ebb and dud

Ray Ragosta

# now and not

```
now  and  not  but  bad  cut  yes  and
cat  and  fat  rat  got  hot  hat  and
yes  the  cow  sat  and  now  sub  tub
yes  cub  cop  put  sad  cow  now  and
mut  bow  wow  bop  lot  how  sly  low
rot  tut  tut  fat  sot  rub  end  pat
gut  not  tot  and  hop  hop  top  dub
yes  and  den  and  lop  mop  rut  pow
pop  mat  hut  jut  all  hap  bat  fop
ass  cot  dot  hub  hub  nub  sop  pub
and  mow  row  tow  yes  sow  cub  tub
and  mop  pop  how  now  bow  wow  not
wry  not  now  and  jot  pot  nut  yes
```

Keith Waldrop

ottos mops trotzt
otto: fort mops fort
ottos mops hopst fort
otto: soso

otto holt koks
otto holt obst
otto horcht
otto: mops mops
otto hofft

ottos mops klopft
otto: komm mops komm
ottos mops kommt
ottos mops kotzt
otto: ogottogott

E. J.

Lulu's pooch droops
Lulu: scoot, pooch, scoot!
Lulu's pooch soon scoots.
Lulu brooms room.

Lulu scoops food.
Lulu spoons roots.
Lulu croons: pooch, pooch.
Lulu broods.

Lulu's pooch drools.
Lulu:poor fool  pooch.
Lulu grooms pooch.

Lulu's pooch poops.
Lulu: oops.

Elizabeth MacKiernan

tat's cat sadly
tat: away cat away
tat's cat swam away
tat: a play

tat had match
tat had hat and fan
tat saw
tat: cat cat
tat wants

tat's cat taps
tat: lap cat lap
tat's cat at hand
tat's cat paws
tat: gad gad gad

Laynie Browne

otto's dog droops
otto: off old dog!
otto's old dog tromps off
otto: oh

otto drops sock
otto drops food
otto stoops
otto: dog! dog!
otto's cool

otto's dog woofs
otto: go dog go!
otto's dog chomps
otto's dog poops
otto: dog got to go

Benjamin Friedlander

Provo's ghost plots
Provo: north ghost north
Provo's ghost plods north
Provo: go-no-go

Provo fools hosts
Provo fools clocks
Provo foxtrots
Provo: ghost ghost
Provo froths

Provo's ghost bops
Provo: stop ghost stop
Provo's ghost stops
Provo's ghost rots
Provo: ovoprovost

Beth Anderson

otto's dog broods
otto: down dog down
otto's dog bows down
otto: goodgood

otto shops for logs
otto shops for corn
otto stops
otto: dog dog
otto looks for comfort

otto's dog knocks
otto: don't go dog don't go
otto's dog won't go
otto's dog poos
otto: ogodogod

                    Martine Bellen




                              Bob's dog flops on porch
                              Bob's dog drools
                              Bob: Poor dog.
                              Bob's dog: Woof!
                              Bob: Now, now.
                              Bob's dog howls
                              Bob: OK, hold on!
                              Bob cooks for dog
                              Bob's dog wolfs down pork chops
                              Bob's dog hops on Bob
                              Bob: Off, boy, off!
                              Bob's dog poops on Bob
                              Bob: Oh God, Oh no, Oh God, Oh.
                              Bob's Mom: Good show, moron.

                                        Leonard Brink

# etüde in f

eile mit feile
eile mit feile
eile mit feile
durch den fald

durch die füste
durch die füste
durch die füste
bläst der find

falfischbauch
falfischbauch

eile mit feile
eile mit feile
auf den fellen
feiter meere

auf den fellen
feiter meere
eile mit feile
auf den fellen

falfischbauch
falfischbauch

eile mit feile
auf den fellen
feiter meere
feiter meere

falfischbauch
falfischbauch
fen ferd ich fiedersehn
falfischbauch
falfischbauch
fen ferd ich fiedersehn
fen ferd ich fiedersehn
falfischbauch
fen ferd ich fiedersehn
falfischbauch
falfischbauch

ach die heimat
ach die heimat
fen ferd ich fiedersehn
ist so feit

E. J.

35

# study in f

hurry up and fate          hurry up and fate
hurry up and fate          favors all on
hurry up and fate          seas so fast
through the foods          seas so fast

through the filed          fails belly
through the filed          fails belly
through the filed          fill I see a fair again
the finned blows          fails belly
                                      fails belly
fails belly                      fill I see a fair again
fails belly                      fill I see a fair again
                                      fails belly
hurry up and fate          fill I see a fair again
hurry up and fate          fails belly
favors all on                  fails belly
seas so fast
                                      home sweet home ah
favors all on                  home sweet home ah
seas so fast                    fill I see a fair again
hurry up and fate          so fairy far
on favors all

fails belly
fails belly

Keith Waldrop

36

## gradus ad parnassum

ding an sich
ding an sich
ding an sich
danke schön

dis an dat
dis an dat
dis an dat
damit nichts

dat's enough
dat's enough

ding an sich
ding an sich
dat's a fella
inna mirra

dat's a fella
inna mirra
ding an sich
dat's a fella

nuff a dat
nuff a dat

ding an sich
dat's a fella
inna mirra
inna mirra

dat's enough
dat's enough
an dat is whad I'm sayin
dat's enough
dat's enough
an dat is whad I'm sayin
an dat is whad I'm sayin
dat's enough
an dat is whad I'm sayin
nuff a dat
nuff a dat

up da creek
up da creek
an dat is whad I'm sayin
widout a paddle

Damon Krukowski

37

fr **o** sch
   **i**

E. J.

```
      i
ch    mp
   o
```

Benjamin Friedlander

```
                              is
                          po      on
                              ti
```

Brian Schorn

```
    o
sh    rt
   i            i                    i
      th   ng        e        bl    nd
         o        bl    nd         a
                     o            James Sherry
```

(Hay fever medication?)

AGHAST

```
              oo
          sn      ze
              ee
```

```
      A
  G       SH
      I
      O
      U
```

Elizabeth MacKiernan

Paul Hoover

```
                              g
                     fr   o
                              ck
              e                     i        k
         fr       t             fr      s
              ui                     e        h
    o
fr      g
   i      ht
```

Laynie Browne

39

|   |   |   |   |   |   |   |   |   |   |   |
|---|---|---|---|---|---|---|---|---|---|---|
| | i | | | | n | | | | u | |
| st | | tch | | bo | | y | | cr | | sh |
| | re | | | | d | | | | a | |
| | ee | | | | a | | | | i | |
| br | | d | | c | | rve | | sw | | tch |
| | ea | | | | u | | | | a | |
| | s | | | | ou | | | | a | |
| re | | olve | | cl | | d | | bl | | nd |
| | v | | | | ue | | | | e | |
| | a | | | | u | | | | a | |
| tr | | ce | | sp | | nk | | gr | | nd |
| | u | | | | a | | | | i | |
| | v | | | | o | | | | u | |
| li | | id | | ch | | ir | | pr | | ne |
| | p | | | | a | | | | o | |
| | a | | | | u | | | | a | |
| sm | | ll | | abo | | t | | st | | rk |
| | e | | | | r | | | | o | |
| | i | | | | ea | | | | a | |
| bl | | nd | | str | | m | | l | | ss |
| | e | | | | u | | | | e | |
| | a | | | | e | | | | a | |
| all | | y | | qu | | ll | | d | | nce |
| | o | | | | i | | | | u | |
| | o | | | | b | | | | g | |
| sh | | ck | | pu | | ic | | vi | | or |
| | a | | | | n | | | | s | |
| | e | | | | au | | | | i | |
| ch | | ck | | st | | nch | | pr | | nce |
| | i | | | | e | | | | a | |
| | a | | | | o | | | | u | |
| gr | | nt | | gr | | ve | | pr | | de |
| | u | | | | a | | | | i | |
| | ea | | | | e | | | | o | |
| app | | se | | dr | | gs | | str | | ng |
| | lau | | | | a | | | | i | |

Elizabeth Fodaski

from: **das grosse e**

e) gegen sechs gehen mehrere mehreren entgegen
gegen zehn stehen mehrere neben mehreren
gegen elf sehen mehrere mehrere stehen
gegen sechs sprechen mehrere gegen mehrere
gegen zehn helfen mehrere mehreren gegen mehrere
gegen elf helfen mehrere mehreren weg
gegen sechs gehen mehrere mehreren entgegen

e) erregendes erregt erregendes
erregtes erregendes erregt erregendes
erregtes erregendes steht erregtem erregenden entgegen
erregtes geht gegen erregtes
versteckendes erregtes bettet steckendes bewegtes erregtes
klebendes wechselt versteckende steckende erregte
bewegte gebettete

e) jeder kennt ehen
neben ehen kennt jeder ehen
neben ehen kennt jeder ehen neben ehen
ehen entstehen eben
ehen entstehen neben ehen
ehen neben ehen enstehen eben neben ehen
ehen geben leben
leben entsteht
leben entsteht nebenher
leben entsteht neben ehen
leben entsteht eben

e) schweres hebt schweres schwerem entgegen
wege legen wege neben wegen weg
lebendes dreht lebendes lebendem entgegen
gestrecktes streckt gestrecktes gestrecktem entgegen
quellen entquellen quellen neben quellen
stellen stellen stellen neben stellen weg
helles bellt hell hellem entgegen
festes presst festes neben festem fest

E. J.

41

from **"the big e"**

e)  even sex-hexed men mend nets
     even zen-spent men need mend
     even elf-seen men bend necks
     even sex-flecked men's seeds fend
     even zen-helped men breed sex seeds
     even elf-helped men tend wrecks
     even sex-hexed men mend nets

e)  errers err re errers
     e'en ere errers err errers erst err'd
     e'en ere errers stretch erect extended
     fete genteel genes effete
     vexed errers better stet bedwetters err'r
     lest vexed errers kept stetted ere bedwetters get better

e)  ever seek ether
     needles even seek ether-seekers
     needles even seek ether needle-seekers seek
     ether evens eden
     ether evens needle-eden
     ether needles ethers even eden-needles seek
     ether greets lechers
     lechers enter
     lechers enter needles even
     lechers enter needle-ether
     lechers enter eden

e)  sweet herbs sweeten sweeter elements
     wet stems whet nettles' wetter welt
     tethers tethered tetherers' tenderer elements
     effected stretches reflect defect tenements
     quellers squelch quellers' nerve-swell
     sellers sell cells' nerve-swelled whey
     hell's belt held helen's element
     feller's press'd-festered neck festers best

Guy Bennett

## the big e

seven's edge the set meets the set
ten's edge the set greets the set
eleven's edge the set sees the set greeted
seven's edge the set vexes the set
ten's edge the set helps the set vex the set
eleven's edge the set helps the set flee
seven's edge the set meets the set

effervescence effervesces effervescence
the effervescent effervescence effervesces effervescence
the effervescent effervescence stems effervescent effervescence
effervescence reverses effervescence
the secret effervescet beds cemented restless effervescence
the cementer tempers the cemented secret restless bedded

the set sees the wedded
except the wedded the set sees the wedded
except the wedded the set sees the wedded except the wedded
the wedded be the wedded
the wedded be the wedded except the wedded
the wedded except the wedded except the wedded be
the wedded send essence
essence the event
essence the event the mere event
essence the event except the wedded
the essence be the essence

swedes swede
swedes swede the set
swedes swede the set steep
swedes term the set steep swede-steep
swedes term the set steel swede-steel
steel feeds the swedes

cell keeps meter teetered vestments
the fettered wrench the metered pens
cell keeps check the best sever scheme

the fettered chew depleted scenes
cell keeps see the fettered scheme the needless trestle
the fettered wreck expected tempests
cell keeps sweep the recent mess
the fettered chew the well-wrecked necks

Lisa Jarnot


### the big e

Gauging sex: hey, may ray-ray, may ray enter-going here?
gouging sane stain, may ray-ray? Nay—mar ray rain.
Go aches elf, say it: "may ray-ray equal Stein?"
Not arranging its raked tour de farce, not arranging arraign-
ment.

Jade her: who can't aim.
An hour who can't blame
aim her who can't jade her
labia start in state
lay burr incite those neighboring
and state—hey babe—aim.

Stroke the stretch, strike streaks, stroke the strike,
straighten stretch, stretch the straight;
wetter stroke over easy
tight.

Quail quote, quell quite, nay—bend quim
up again
fested feisty, festive presto, upper theory
hello below
hail both
hail fellow to follow
well fast.

Rachel Blau DuPlessis

### elected e

seven precedes eleven
ever precedes never
bet precedes debt
bedded precedes wedded
elves engender evergreens

peter sees the swede
even her sweet verses end
the wretch stretches the vetch
stretched verses flex
he enters the deep end

well met when wet
the set tempers the fête
seven verses end eleven hexes
ever the lever
sets the temper

her pet stretches the net
the bee is hexed
the beetle flees the hex
yet gets the next jet
the hex flexes

enter zed
her red pet fed red beets hexes the verse
eleven bees eke effects
sevens sever the jet
steve pees

elves effervesce
effete elks elect egrets
eggs seek egress
see eve eschew essence
everest precedes eden

ellen pressed efferent elements
ejected the eldest
gene met the echt hexed bell
else the elm's embers enmesh ephebes
dexter edges express endless entente

lee errs
helen's ex the pest ebbs
ewes expect excellent ether
excel except when erect
eh

enter the empress
esteemed entrée
ecce ernest
excretes expense
etc

Ed's well-heeled eels emerge
where the emcee embezzles emblems
emends the ensemble
fetters esteem
etches the entrenched epée

the extent repels
expresses extreme pretense
exerts exempt excrescences
excess excrement exceeds events
extends excerpts

experts expel excellence except exegeses
set seven steps three ems deep
let the verse be stretched
severed yes
streets sleep

be ended

Keith Waldrop

### ere we were jelled

We ended "eye" (see: jewelry) & lewd
mêlées. There's the reckless
eggshell present, Helen's severe
new deeds, the ever self-
defended streets.

Heedless, she senselessly beseeched teen
egrets, helped them wend, sexless, endlessly preened. Seven never
nested, grew beveled, demented, beepers prevented, they were
betterment pretenders. Eleven blended pretext & nerve, neglected
bezels & needled weekenders endlessly. He
tells me, "here, be these
every embers
where the next yes sleeps, deep,
melded." The pecker! (Here, the leper meets the legless meddler.)

We'll deed the been-seen. Even
red gently wedges between Western shells
secretly when he sees her.

Remember Bethlehem, the next December? When we were
between-decks, presented
the perfect letterpressed penny, he fell,
weed-free; feet met heels—he reeled. She, the expert sweet
pepper, blew these beserk twelve per
cent events, where? When we were sent peerless
blessedness elements, she defended me, *démence de* berets, best-
sellers, Greeks.

Prefect, tell me, where excellent
dresses be excess?
We're grey-eyed, lessened, feeble; yet when
the here fell, we were
there. We wrestled the few
French legends left; then we rested.

Eleni Sikelianos

## the big eclipse

"The go on to          go to meet
        here          stand next
is the word               see
for word      counting      talk against
                          help against
                          go" ———


toward something everyone beside couples life
something roads springs places something

[the pretend body of the poem's other body
                counter body
Body of regard          already more time has been
spent counting than recounting]

something toward something places something(
something happens where something happened(
something was someone walking a wide perimeter around
                                        someone's
something's someone is someone's somewhat
something's method is not reducible to someone
something towards might move something towards

toward limit's interest moves something toward

each step of the way

the several number of none
counting the exciting excited conjugation of something
enumeration happens everyone knows number beside number
makes couple makes enunciation of numeral
beside the side-effect of one just happens repetition

infinitely something hold places for somethings

finally something eradicates something without conclusion
bright brightly springs at horizon's furthest cuticle one letter
moon, sun, or another firmly
posits the fiction of actual disappearance

one letter is as place amulet against stampede of letters pressing
to spell themselves again into something

Susan Gevirtz

### discourse A

time A      again agon unchained to gain a gain of more and more
time A1   the fun the fun the fun of more and more and more
time A2   sweet etude in A to spritz the air with ritzy fits of more
            and more and more and more and more
time A3   sweet sweet esprit pure perfidy unbridled sprees in
            threes of more and more and more and more and more
            and more
time A4   not for remorse not to deplore refrains refrains of all
            that strains toward more and more and more and more
            and more and more and more
time A5   ah what a time to be alive a big high-five for more of
            more and more and more and more and more and
            more and more and more

Joan Retallack

# the late tale

then several (like five) venture there
(site: transparent teal blue plane)
maybe meet several (like nine) more
then several (more like ten)
gather their flesh outside
(nerve directions: encase)
erect spines near several others
then several (imagine eleven)
see several others being erect (maybe noble)
then five (maybe seven) chatter
opposite downtrodden eight (maybe less)
then maybe less help maybe more
duel several others (maybe even more)
then the *then* dwindles beside the *the*
leaving even less gathered
none erect
then the superbly sculpted supine figures
(imagine neat pile)
are raised
open-mouthed because haunted
then the several open-mouthed
but haunted figures venture
near quiet abodes
(they penetrate cement castles, insect domiciles)
then several armed (some men)
dangle celery before children
dressed like donkeys (possible sacrifice?)
then the donkeys (maybe they are children)
shed their purple capes
before fleeing their haunted parents
then more meet less even then the less faces more
then the darkness divides itself
releasing molten red cascade
fiery tongues descend
demanding more than donkies
then the donkeys aren't children anymore
because different celestial effects

infect their heads
then the dreamers
(imagine one maybe three)
tell their tale near the fire
then the tale (maybe more)
explodes above the telling
then the donkeys
(are they haunted children?)
slide like stale bubbled cream
inside the children
their red smiles
then the disguised children descend
demanding larger purple capes
then several more stories are told beside the fire
then these stories
unable to extinguish the stories preceding them
(note: noises (notes)
begin breaking
ice clogged lake,
teal green plane)
because each tries extinguishing the others
their frozen syllables dissolve
more tales
(are they holes?
are they moles?)
emerge
then several marriages break
leaving the children to wander
then the wandering comets
(imagine children) return
their blue stones exciting
the cimmerian darkness
then several figures
(some are comets,
others are children)
converge inside the wooden abode
(termite eaten table?
rotted cellar beams?
master's teak-lined bedroom?)

where the dreamer
leaves the dream
others seek
believing therein lies the answer
forgetting they have the lake
the ice
the comet
the red stone
then the answer becomes the little haunted question
(imagine comet)
suspended above the lacustrine drinker
(green marble statue)
then once more the *then*
begins breaking factories
little sweatshops crammed together
the children swear opposite the donkeys
the donkeys are secretly infidels
dipguised hermits
large drudge machines
they (donkeys perhaps children) become heroes
when they reduce their drivel quotient
then the children hidden inside the donkies
begin exhausting their parents
several disinherit their progeny
others take downhearted hikes
then the ice age begins once more
(maybe twice)
then the children are cooled inside the frozen lake machine
the parents become delirious
(huge venomous parties)
the donkeys are freed
everyone rejoices
then  the donkeys make their mistake
they dance beside the fire
then several (maybe more) meet several others
(some venture where *there*
they once gathered erect)
then the celestial delivery systems begin their bombardment
then the here (imagine infinite more) empties itself

before the darkness becomes the emblazoned shield
whose foretelling occurred
(inside the faded flame once called *time*)
when the tale began loosening the blackened tiles
lodged inside the infinitely broken sea

John Yau

### free e's

We need red keys,
        yet ten femme clever levers mess free beds.
We remember greed — Jeff's next level text eyes the nerd mess.
Deer knees bleed evenly —
Vets beg eels eyes.
Cree reed webs eek senneted seeds — even better bedded.
Lee needs even keel-creeds, sees netted mermen.
Mermen kneel erect — even keels elected me.
R. E. R. jellee legs greet eyes.
Ether net egresses eek regs even yet.

Lee Ann Brown

from **gestures : a game**

        weather ye poses


     **anglican**
            **for a piss-hop**


     **bluesy**
   **b**   **lues**   **y**
  **b**    **lues**     **y**
 **b**      **lues**       **y**

E. J.

```
        crawl
     c   raw  l
   c     raw     l
 c       raw        l

        champ
     c  ham  p
   c    ham     p
 c      ham        p
```

R. W.


**a romance**

```
          frank
       f  ran  k
     f    ran    k
   f      ran      k

          after

          sally
       s  all  y
     s    all    y
   s      all      y

          day
```

Brian Schorn

**seif**

**roh**

E. J.

beg

lad

R. W.

| | |
|---|---|
| dealer | cryptic |
| rant | on |
| | |
| deal | crypt |
| errant | icon |
| ———— | ———— |
| | |
| total | barb |
| lure | lab |
| | |
| tot | bar |
| allure | blab |
| ———— | ———— |
| | |
| justice | barb |
| cream | anal |
| | |
| just | bar |
| ice cream | banal |
| ———— | ———— |
| | |
| grain | barb |
| year | aster |
| | |
| grainy | bar |
| ear | baster |
| ———— | ———— |
| | |
| your | barb |
| ankle | eagle |
| | |
| you | bar |
| rankle | beagle |

Ray Ragosta

```
tee        :    ein stück


           :
           :
lieber     :    tee
           :


[egal]     :
   ich     :    tee
           :


           :
 fragt     :
[er nie]   :    tee
           :
```

E. J.

**MY : T**

```
            :
   liber  :  tea
            :

   [fr]   :
 eterni  :  tee
            :

  [equ]  :
   all a  :  tease
            :
```

**TEA : TOTAL**

```
            :
   tee   :  nsy
            :


            :
   tee   :  tering
            :


            :
   tea   :  sea
            :  [fly]
            :
```

Craig Watson

## TAY : A PLAY

```
      :
  en  T  ray
      :


      :
 dan  T  ay
      :


      :
delec T  ay
      :
```

## T : A MEAL

```
m i g h T e e e e e

   bi T e e e e

    i Tee e

      Tee

       b
       o
       n
       e
```

Craig Watson

**tea** : **a piece**

  :
  :
lovely : tea
  :

  :
[Equal] :
  in : tea
  :

  :
fuckt :
Ernie : tea
  :


**teen** : **i'm stuck**

  :
  :
libber : teen
  :

  :
[ay gal] :
  ick! : teen
  :

  :
fract(al) :
earning : teen
  :

Lee Ann Brown

# fortschreitende räude

him hanfang war das wort hund das wort war bei
gott hund gott war das wort hund das wort hist fleisch
geworden hund hat hunter huns gewohnt


him hanflang war das wort hund das wort war blei
flott hund flott war das wort hund das wort hist fleisch
gewlorden hund hat hunter huns gewlohnt


schim schanflang war das wort schund das wort war blei
flott schund flott war das wort schund das wort schist fleisch
gewlorden schund schat schunter schuns gewlohnt


schim schanschlang schar das wort schlund schasch wort
schar schlei schlott schund flott war das wort schund
schasch fort schist schleisch schleschlorden schund
schat schlunter schluns scheschlohnt


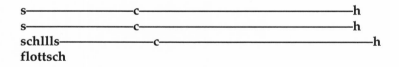

s—————————c—————————————h
s—————————c—————————————h
schllls—————————c—————————————h
flottsch

E. J.

# progressive sin

sin the besinning was the sword and the sword was with
god and god was the sword and the sword has flesh
become and has among us dwelled

sin the besinning wash the sword sand the sword wash with
got sand got wash the sword sand the sword hash flesh
besome sand hash among pus dwelled

sin the be sing wash the sword sand the sword wash wits
gut sand gut wash the sword sand the sword hash fish
be some sand hash song pus dwelled

sin he be sin sin was he or an he or ash its
gut an gut ash he or and he or ash is
be so and ash son pus led

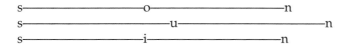

Craig Watson

# foul vowels

on thi bigonnong wes thi wurd end thi wurd wes woth
gud end gud wes thi wurd end thi wurd hes flish
bicumi end hes emung as dwillid


un tho bogunning wis tho ward ind tho ward wis wuth
gad ind gad wis tho ward ind tho ward his flosh
bocamo ind his imang es dwollod


an thu bugannang wos thu werd ond thu werd wos wath
ged ond ged wos thu werd ond thu werd hos flush
bucemu ond hos omeng is dwullud


en tha bagenneng wus tha wird und tha wird wus weth
gid und gid wus tha wird und tha wird hus flash
bacima und hus uming os dwallad


in the beginning was the word and the word was with
god and god was the word and the word has flesh
become and has among us dwelled


Craig Watson

## progressive mange

Skin the beginning was the Word, and the Word was with God, and the Word was God.
The same was skin the beginning with God.
All things were made by him; and without him not any thing made that was made.


Skin the beginning was the Word, and the Word was with prod, and the Word was prod.
The same was skin the beginning with prod.
All things were made by whim; and without whim not any thing made that was made.


Skin ape beginning was ape Word, and ape Word was with prod, and ape Word was prod.
Ape same was skin ape beginning with prod.
All apings were made by whim; and without whim not any aping made a pat was made.


Skin ape beginning was ape Word, bland ape Word was with prod, bland ape Word was prod.
Ape same was skin ape beginning with prod.
All apings were made by whim; bland without whim not any aping made a pat was made.


Skin ape beginning wash ape Word, bland ape Word wash with prod, bland ape Word wash prod.
Ape shame wash skin ape beginning with prod.
All apings were made by whim; bland without whim not any aping made a pat wash made.


Ray Ragosta

## GOD-DOG-it! (wherein and = GOD backwards, and things just keep back tracking from there)

When all things began, the word already was. The Word dwelt with GOD, and what GOD was, the Word was. The Word, then, was GOD at the beginning, and through him all things came to be; no single thing was created without him.

When all things began, the word already was. The Word dwelt with GOD, DOG what GOD was, the Word was. The Word, then, was GOD at the beginning, DOG through him all things came to be; no single thing was created without him.

When all things began, the DrOwG already was. The DrOwG dwelt with GOD, DOG what GOD was, the DrOwG was. The DrOwG, then, was GOD at the beginning, DOG through him all things came to be; no single thing was created without him.

When all things began, the DrOwG already saw. The DrOwG dwelt with GOD, saw DOG at the beginning, through him all things came to be; no single thing saw created without him.

When all things began, the DrOwG already sawed GOD. The DrOwG dwelt with G/OD, D/OG what sawed G/OD. The DrOwG, then, sawed through h/i/m all things; no single thing saw created without h/i/m.

"No single thing" sawed "When all things began." The DrOwG sawed D/OG dwelt through h/i/m, without h/i/m. Sawed D/OG dwelt smelt, then, through all things. No DrOwG thing saw created when single things /gan to /be.

Tina Darragh

# INTERLUDE:

# IMITATIONS AT LARGE

## Nothing

*for Ernst Jandl*

→
↓

| | |
|---|---|
| Mir fällt jetzt nichts ein | (Emir felt jets Nick's ion) |
| Nothing falls into me right now | ——— |
| Rien ne me tombe dedans à présent | (Irene née me tomb deadens a present) |
| Nichts fällt mir herein in der Gegenwart | (Niches felt mere harangue in the gag and wart) |
| Nothing falls for me in the present | ——— |
| Nichts fällt für mich im Geschenk | (night's phallus for me in a gay shank) |

Anne Tardos

fiolets for Efe
ify vor Fiolet

Efe infests her money
Fiolet gets diffidends

fat 69 vor Efe
firgin vor Fiolet

Fiolet's a vast woman
Efe is nice to a vault

firility vor Fiolet
fagabonds vor Efe

Efe rents a fan
and mofes to the fillage

Fiolet vends vor herselv
and vain would lie down

**1 and 5 and a german
accent**


fun faltz
wife woxtrots

fun warmhand
wife wallows

fun wallguy
wife fills to power



R. W.


**s'**

ill well ills well ills wells sill well sill swell sills swell sills swells
i'll well i'lls well i'lls wells si'll well si'll swell si'lls swell si'lls swells
ill we'll ills we'll ills we'lls sill we'll sill swe'll sills swe'll sills swe'lls
i'll we'll i'lls we'll i'lls we'lls si'll we'll si'll swe'll si'lls swe'll si'lls swe'lls

Brian Schorn

**for breakfast**

too many jelly do    nuts
            UGH

**bookshop**

die book hand lung
bie hook land dung
hie look dand bung
lie dook band hung

```
MOR          GUE
PRO   TON    ITE
CAN          SIL
```

P  O  _V_  E ⌐T R¬ Y     _tr._

**Louis: Kings of France**

```
              I
              II
              III
              I   V
                  V
              V   I
              V   II
              V   III
              I          X
                         X
                         X   I
                         X   II
                         X   III
                         X   I   V
                         X       V
                         X       V  I
                         X       V  II
                         X       V  III
```

**alchemy**

g
  older
p
  older
b
  older
f
  older
c
  older
h
  older
s

Brian Schorn

# II

# ORIGINALS & APPROXIMATIONS

# chanson

l'amour
die tür
the chair
der bauch

the chair
die tür
l'amour
der bauch

der bauch
die tür
the chair
l'amour

l'amour
die tür
the chair

le tür
d'amour
der chair
the bauch

le chair
der tür
die bauch
th'amour

le bauch
th'amour
die chair
der tür

l'amour
die tür
the chair

am'lour
tie dür
che thair
ber dauch

tie dair
che lauch
am thür
ber'dour

che dauch
am'thour
ber dür
tie lair

l'amour
die tür
the chair

E. J.

pi
  ano
  anino
  anissimo

pi
pi

o
  nano
  nanino
  nanissimo

o
pi

.

E. J.

# calypso

ich was not yet
in brasilien
nach brasilien
wulld ich laik du go

wer de wimen
arr so ander
so quait ander
denn anderwo

ich was not yet
in brasilien
nach brasilien
wulld ich laik du go

als ich anderschdehn
mange lanquidsch
will ich anderschdehn
auch lanquidsch in rioo

ich was not yet
in brasilien
nach brasilien
wulld ich laik du go

wenn de senden
mi across de meer
wai mi not senden wer
ich wulld ich laik du go

yes yes de senden
mi across de meer
wer ich was not yet
ich laik du go sehr

ich was not yet
in brasilien
yes nach brasilien
wulld ich laik du go

E. J.

### 16 yearth old

thickthteen yearth
thouth thtation
what ith
what ith
he thppothed to do
thouth thtation
thickthteen yearth
what ith
what ith
that boy
what ith
he thppothed to do
what ith
what ith
he thppothed to do
thickthteen yearth
thouth thtation
what ith
he thppothed to do
that boy
with hith
thickthteen yearth

R. W.

schtzngrmm
schtzngrmm
t-t-t-t
t-t-t-t
grrrmmmmm
t-t-t-t
s————c————h
tzngrmm
tzngrmm
tzngrmm
grrrmmmmm
schtzn
schtzn
schtzngrmm
schtzngrmm
tssssssssssssssssss
grrt
grrrrrt
grrrrrrrrrt
scht
scht
t-t-t-t-t-t-t-t-t
scht
tzngrmm
tzngrmm
t-t-t-t-t-t-t-t-t
scht
scht
scht
scht
scht
grrrrrrrrrrrrrrrrrrrr
t-tt

E. J.

[*Schützengraben* = trench; there are no vowels because "war does not sing."]

```
                uncle tom's cabin
                 ncle tom's cabi
                  cle tom's cab
                   le tom's ca
                    e tom's c
                     tom's
                    sssssssss
         aaaaaaaaaaaaaaaaaaaaa
                      t
                        o
                      t
                        o
                          m
                      t
```

E. J.

## double choir

it man playest our women with only reedorgan
walkest on fingertipsiest and past.
it woman playest our men with only clarinestlings
buttonest up and blowest an ever song over.
it man playest our women with only mythorgan
lockest up and whistlest nuzzlemuzzle.
it woman playest our men with only it am a violiner
gettest up a condoctor and unwrappest the orgastra.

R. W.

## seven little stories

there once was a man named THOMAS. he bent his knee. "you bend your knee," said his woman. "and how," replied the man, "long is it going to rain I'd like to know."

there once was a man named JACOB. "excuse me," he said to his woman, "you're dirty." "where shall we?" asked the woman.

"what shall i do? what shall i do? what shall i do?" the man named ZEBORIUS was asked by his woman. "do," explained ZEBORIUS, "you love me?"

there once was a man named NEPOMUK. his woman asked: "what time is it? what time is it?" "half," said NEPOMUK, "i not told you not to bozzer me?"

there once was a man named THADDEUS, whose woman asked: "what consistency is it?" "goo," said THADDEUS modestly, 'dnight."

"where is it? where is it? where is it?"rich JONATHAN was asked by his woman. "under," replied the rich man, "no condition will I tell you."

there once was a man named PETER. "what time is it? what time is it?" asked his woman. "ell," said PETER oddly, "even."

R. W.

80

niagaaaaaaaaaaaaaaaa

        ra fell

niagaaaaaaaaaaaaaaaa

        ra fell

R. W.

england is low and gray. everything in england is low and gray. but everything gray in england is green and that's the great thing about it. everything in england is low and gray. but everything low is an anchor of the sky over england. that's the great thing about it.

england is. that is its history. that is english history. england is low and gray is not its history, but the great thing about it. that is the great thing about its history.
england is. not elizabeth i not john landless not attlee not canute not lionheart are its history. england is is its history. english history. everything else is heartless circulation.

green is the english gray. and what a green. blue [and what a blue] is the gray of the green sky over england. red is the gray of the blue green of the red-red mailbox pillars at the corners, and the gardens [and what gardens] are gardengray in all ardent shades of gray—in red-red green and yellow-gray garden spring-times.

a fall path leads to summer, and a guy makes a fallguy out of wrinkles. summer makes wrinkles out of a guy, and fall makes a path for the guy out of wrinkles. now only a fall path leads to summer, the guy out of wrinkles has counted on wrinkles, but the girls are as much make-up as leaves on the hands of fall, and that's a lot, especially in the avenue.

you are an english girl is a thought, not a possible form of address. but we think at a distance. so we think at a distance: she is an english girl.
she is an english girl is a thought, not a possible form of address. we're not talking anyway, we're just thinking. she is a pretty english girl is a prettier thought.

england is not an angler, but it has its catches. these are spread over the country as in a fishnet. it is the largest fishnet of which you can say: it has its catches, its matches. the ropes are knotted properly but not tight. herrings, too, love life and fight for it. england is not an angler, but has few spirals.

a mountain is a real mountain only as a lonely fish. a lonely fish among lonely fish: they hold each other's fin, but never rub shoulders or sniff. their mouths are not oiled, their eyes dry. their language is the sign language of loneliness, barren ice, expectant rubble, stone by stone.

the tourist buys a ticket to the museum of the alps, where poking is permitted, and a catalogue in his language. in the museum, the tourist puts on his catalogue as spectacles, climbs an exhibited mountain and with inexplicable success pokes the back of this fish. in the pendulum clock he carries, the tourist functions as a perfect edelweiss pendulum for which left equals right between the bank of england and an airy pound-sterling-meadow. but it's the alpenstock he shows off to his friends.

england used to be a rose or hatbox. but now there's a parting of ways, and under ambling hoofs we hear a crunch as of pearls. amblers are easily distracted, but also a tough mass, a glue to mend the broken teacup.
pearls go on crunching the farther the amblers amble, and the farther the amblers amble with pearls crunching under their hoofs the more popular the gestures of the poplars. lizard-tongued lilac hisses along the fence that runs around the garden, overheating, in shorts, training for the olympics.
when the teacup breaks a memory may cling to the crack of mended damage and thus fasten the handle.

england used to be a rose satellite of a hatbox. but the baron, who in the form of hundreds of overturned iron chairs knelt all through the hyde-park-winter at the edge of the artificial lake, has turned into autumn. on his mouse-gray skin, march turbines are opening their greedy beaks. reporters appear with starved cameras on a leash and wait for the revolution of the masses of grasses. we are the first clarinets of this springtime, says black-bird to blackbird.

england used to be a hat without thorns, a rose in a box. but what would become of the tv towers sticking their hatpins into the horizon if the rust-red dog wallops from wales had no teeth left for cow feet. therefore the legs of the owners of the rust-red dog wallops from wales and the lower legs of the wives of the owners of the rust-red dog wallops from wales turn into cow feet and will go on turning into cow feet as long as the rust-red dog wallops from wales have teeth left. don't be afraid, they only nibble. this explains the use of rust-red dog wallops in wales where there are cows.

churchill ran ahead and
stumbled over his hands

churchill as churchill sat in his coat next to his wife mrs. churchill in the theater and looked into the theater. churchill in his coat was not yet sitting in his coat next to his wife mrs.churchill in the theater and looking into the theater when he looked through the door of the theater into the theater and walked through the door and through the door among bows and through the hall and through the door next to his wife mrs. churchill, but through the narrow door ahead of his wife mrs. churchill, and through the hall among bows walked through the theater and looked into the theater while the gentlemen and ladies and young people were no longer sitting, not because they knew that churchill in his coat next to his wife mrs. churchill was entering the theater and look-ing, they were standing because they saw or had been told and therefore knew that churchill in his coat next to his wife mrs. churchill had looked through the door of the theater into the theater and had entered through the door and walked among bows through the door and through the hall and through the door next to his wife mrs. churchill, but through the narrow door ahead of his wife mrs. churchill, and had walked among bows through the hall through the theater and had looked into the theater and was right now in his coat next to his wife mrs. churchill walking up the aisle between the seats to the right and left where the gentlemen and ladies and young people had been sitting before they stood up and clapped their hands and was now sitting down inhis coat in the fourth row on the right to the left of his wife mrs. churchill, but had turned around in his coat before he sat down to the left of his wife mrs. churchill and greeted the gentlemen and ladies and young people who stood and clapped with his sign which is the victory-v with two fingers. then churchill as churchill and not as sir winston not yet as sir winston sat in his coat in his seat next to his wife mrs. churchill in the theater and looked into the theater and the performance began.

england used to be a gland without n, a nut without doe, a duck without donald or xylophone, a trip gone astray without snails. for three days, however, several seventeen tennisballs have been dancing on little felt toes and here and there lost a lemon. to see this spectacle, golf clubs, confessionals and knee warmers are arriving from near and far.

every englishman has form. hence various englishmen have various forms, many englishmen have many forms, and all englishmen do certainly not have all forms, but still a great many. certain englishmen have certain forms, and various englishmen have many, many have many various forms, variously same and various variously many. many englishmen have manners, hat brims, dirty fingernails, mosquito bites, uppercrusts, and some have shingles. many have noses. many noses of various englishmen have various forms, but one single formula: kleenex. on different days four different englishmen have four noses, but a single formula: kleenex. one single englishman has many different noses in one single formula, but only one single nose in the formula: kleenex. so every englishman has formulas. so various englishmen have various formulas, many englishmen have many formulas, and blue englishmen do certainly not all have blue formulas, but many do. so all englishmen have many various forms and formulas, but while no single englishman has the same form as another single englishman, of all englishmen all have of all the many various formulas of all englishmen all a single one: half a double is a whole. half a double englishman is a whole, and what englishman would not be an englishman as a whole, so what englishman would not be

half a double as an englishman and as a whole? many english-
men have manners, hat brims, dirty fingernails, mosquito bites,
uppercrusts, and some have shingles. but what englishman
would not rather be half a double than no whole? so all english-
men have of all the many various formulas of all englishmen all
a single one: half a double is a whole. a double half is likewise a
whole, not an exception that proves the rule. half a triple is a
whole and a half, but not an exception that proves the rule. no
half, however, is an englishman but only a whole. so half a triple
is only a single englishman and a half. a half, however, is no
englishman. a double half triple, however, is three times a whole.
so englishmen stand in the pub and have noses.

london is a tube of toothpaste. this is why visitors bring their
toothbrushes. london is a tube of toothpaste that one man has
resting on a bed of porcelain over which the other stumbles when
his fingertips go for a walk in the thunder jug.
but all happiness has limits, and out of the scented tombs of the
perfumeries arise toothpaste mummies in tubes, none of which
tubes is london. the bakers have white hands, the farmers have
the seed, but the asphalt acrobat does not even want to be free of
his chains, but rather to pull coins out of skinflints by constrict-
ing himself more and more tightly in his iron boa. adam already
knew this trick, lay down on the ironing board and dried the
sweat of his brow. let's make it hot for him, say the skinflints,
who melt coppers down into lumps of gold and beer bottles, let's
make it hot for him till his chains evaporate. but all happiness has
limits, the dentures of the barges chew stale thames water, a bus
may jump, and bridges unfold.

a collision with a child under it is a gull preaching whitish-gray
peace to the red dean. but not all vehicles have wings, not even
the lean ones. bones give them a piece of their mind, tinny ones
wave tin hats, meaty ones roll meatballs. when it comes to a col-
lision, there is a child under every blotter, but the red dean claims
it's just a grease spot and continues to elbow into prayer. the
gulls live in angular rooms and at night close their eyes with
chewing gum.

most architects are architects like most. but some architects are architects like very few architects. these are uncommon architects. most architects want to build as much as possible. these are the common architects. most are like this. a few architects build most. these are the most successful architects. these are the richest. very few architects do not want to build anything. those are the most uncommon architects. lemon trees do not blossom lemons. also, lemons are not architects. yet most people have tasted lemonade, for lemonade is compatible with architecture. only very few architects are unfamiliar with lemons or do not want to build anything. but lemon trees are most eager. only, most architects do not blossom lemons. but most architects are not lemontrees either. it is often said that england is a big violet lemon in a hatbox at five meters' distance from an architect and that london is the toothpaste tube of this violet lemon.

short young men place their heads under hovering magnetic bearskin caps. the earth fastens suction cups on their soles. the hovering magnetic bearskin caps pull the short young men upward. the short young men's mothers are pleased: so he isn't so antimagnetic after all. the bearskin caps pull the young men upward and elongate them while the young men's soles stick stamps onto the earth. when the bearskin caps fit the elongated young men they swear a solemn oath never to spit into the mouth organ that houses the big sad king they guard. whereupon most of them learn to play the penny organ and hang their mouth organ up on the heart of a junk-dealer.

a tiny wet water-lily climbed the seven rungs of the moon. under the cupola of st. paul's cathedral it whispered: are you the whispering gallery? yes, whispered the whispering gallery.

R. W.

stilton cheese
cureth
warts
wormeth
through needles
calleth
BBC
moist soulful

E. J.

awholelavatoryawholelavatoryawholelavatoryawholelav
atoryawholelavatoryawholelavatoryawholelavatoryaw
holelavatoryawholelavatoryawholelavatoryawholel
avatoryawholelavatoryawholelavatoryawholela
vatoryawholelavatoryawholelavatory
heavenprotectmefromsomuchwater

R. W.

ric
ric
ric
lyyyyyyyyyyy

gic
gic
gic
traaaaaaaaaaa

lick
lick
lick
gaaaaaaaaaaar

pick
pick
pick
tooooooooooth

R. W.

| **1944** | **1945** |
|----------|----------|
| war | war |
| war | war |
| war | war |
| war | war |
| war | may |
| war | |
| war | |
| war | |
| war | |
| war | |
| war | |
| war | |

(marking a turn)

R. W.

# **portrait of a girl**

blond

bl11111111111111111111111111111111111111111111111
ue-eyed

```
                                              s
                                             /
                                            /
                                           /
                                          /
                                         /
                                        /
                          s
                         /
                        /
                       /
                      /
                  s
                 /
                /
           s
          /
sssssssssss
```

iren e

s
   and
       s
   and
s
   and
       s
   and
s
   and
       s
   and
s
   and

R. W.

### third try successful

```
          to                        his
he tries              bulthroughlet
          put a                     brain


          to                        his
he tries              bthurloulghet
          put a                     brain

                      a
he puts                             bburlalient
              through his
```

R. W.

## surface translation

my hear leaps up when i behold
a rainbow in the sky
so was it when my life began
so is it now i am a man
so be it when i shall grow old
or let me die!
the child is father of the man
and i could wish my days to be
bound each to each by natural piety

(william wordsworth)


mai hart lieb zapfen eibe hold
er renn bohr in sees kai
so was sieht wenn mai läuft begehen
so es sieht nahe emma mähen
so biet wenn ärschel grollt
ohr leck mit ei!
seht steil dies fader rosse mähen
in teig kurt wisch mai desto bier
baum deutsche deutsch bajonett schur alp eiertier

E. J.

## poggish

the pog
qarks
qites
dants
anp
disses

R. W.

al
pha
bet
cal
pha
det
el
pha
fet
gal
pha
het
il
pha
jet
kal
pha
let
mal
pha
net
ol
pha
pet
qual
pha
ret
sal
pha
tet
ul
pha
vet
wal
pha
xet
yl
pha
zet

E. J.

no

no

no

no

no

no

no

(answers to seven unasked questions)

E. J.

## flamingo

```
flam            men
     in
        go  home
              men  only
        go  home
     in
flam            men
```

E. J.

[*flammen* = flames]

## hike

from from        to to
from to          to from

from from to from

from from        to to

from to to to

from to          to from
from from        to to


and back

R. W.

## sundial

```
/ u n d i a l
s / n d i a l
s u / d i a l
s u n / i a l
s u n d / a l
s u n d i / l
s u n d i a /
```

E. J.

**séance**

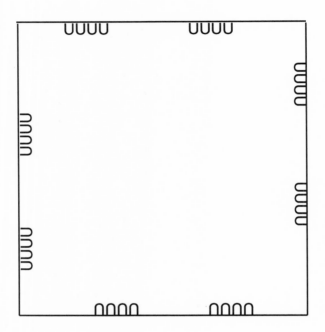

E. J.

by god!

or a bit above

R. W.

# what you can do without vowels

kss

fck

lck

sck

pss

sht

E. J.

**the british ambassador**

such
a
mess

at
my
age

what
a
message

E. J.

## every man his own edison

in the nest of taughtology
every man feels comfy. clautomation
promises a lifelong hold. powerology
is the only science. telephant
carries everyone to everyone, telepower
likewise. lyrkitsch and sickophone
occupy glands and ears. decorations of quarcinoma
are handed out by the president of the you know what.

R. W.

## in god

that he believed in god once had
truly he not could say
there simply been god there
and then there no longer been god there
and inbetween nothing
but now he would truly find it a stretch
to in god believe now
however no one could guarantee
that perhaps one day
god would simply there be again
and inbetween nothing

Anselm Hollo

## consultation

doctor i no can stop shitting
you me give drug for stop shitting

doctor i no can stop saying ouch ouch
you me give drug for stop saying ouch ouch

doctor i no can stop talk in head
    when want go sleep
you me give drug for stop talk in head
    and go sleep

doctor i no can stop croaking
you me give drug for croaking

Anselm Hollo

### to existence

to existence
add coexistence
and why not to coexistence
cocoexistence
and then to that
cococoexistence
whose logical extension
is cocococoexistence

thus there are no limits to co
whatsoever
no limits to weapons systems
the prerequisite for such co
but only to existence
which occurs only once in each instance
and hence is so inconsequential

Anselm Hollo

## august stramm

he august stramm
abbreviated has
german poem much

him august stramm
abbreviated has
world war one

we however have
had a little longer
to run off at the mouth

Anselm Hollo

...said he had always had something to say, and had always known that one could say it this way and that way and that way; so had never had to struggle to say something but always with the way of saying it. for in what you have to say you have no alternative, but in the way of saying it you have an uncertain number of possibilities. there are poets who say all sorts of things and always in the same way. this had never attracted him, after all there is only one thing you have to say, but this one thing again and again and always in a new way.

R. W.

NOTE:

Ernst Jandl was born in 1925 in Vienna where he still lives. He began publishing poems in 1956 and quickly attracted attention as the wittiest and most exuberant of experimental poets, with a knack for uncovering the comic potential in discrepancies between sound and spelling, in clichés, mispronunciations, dialect etc. Readers with a bit of German will enjoy his 'surface translation' of "My heart leaps up when I behold." He has not only explored the limits of language in his visual and sound poems, but also social and political borders by using *Ausländerdeutsch*, the kind of pidgin German spoken by foreign workers.

Aside from poems he has written radio plays, some of them in collaboration with Friederike Mayröcker, and poetological texts (*Die schöne Kunst des Schreibens*, 1976; *Das Öffnen und Schliessen des Mundes*, 1985). He has trans- lated Gertrude Stein, Robert Creeley's *The Island*, and John Cage's *Silence*.

Among his many prestigious literary prizes in both Austria and Germany are the Georg-Trakl-Preis (1974), Georg-Büchner-Preis and Grosser Österreichischer Staatspreis (both 1984).


Michael Hamburger has translated a different selec- tion of poems by Ernst Jandl: *Dingfest/Thingsure,* Dublin: Dedalus Press, 1997. This volume also contains an excel- lent introduction to Jandl's work.